Future
Anthropology

Future Anthropology

Science
Fiction
Poems

Jean-Paul L. Garnier

Introduction by Bryan Thao Worra

SPACE COWBOY BOOKS

SPACE COWBOY BOOKS
61871 Twentynine Palms Hwy.
Joshua Tree, CA 92252
www.spacecowboybooks.com

Future Anthropology
ISBN# 978-1-732-82571-0

First Edition | 2019
Cover Art and illustrations by Zara Kand
Book design by Jon Christopher

This book is dedicated to **R. Soos** for all that he has done for the poets of the Morongo Basin and across the world. Thank you for making dreams come true and for bringing the poetic community together.

Future Anthropology, Speculative Verse and beyond.

The Russian poet Yevgeny Yevtushenko, in his poem "People" once noted that no people were uninteresting. "Their fate is like the chronicle of planets. / Nothing in them is not particular, / and planet is dissimilar from planet." Contemplating our collective mortality he goes on to note the worlds that die within us, and "There are left books and bridges / and painted canvas and machinery / Whose fate is to survive." This weighs on my mind as I look through the assembled poems in *Future Anthropology*, appraising it through many lenses as a reader, but particularly this year as the President of Science Fiction and Fantasy Poetry Association, an international society in over 19 nations committed to what is presently known as speculative poetry. That is to say, poetry engaged to varying degrees with the themes and elements of science fiction, fantasy, horror, and other deeply imaginative genres. There are some who take issue with that definition. There are always people who take issue with a definition. But it's a start. To its credit, the Science Fiction and Fantasy Poetry Association has found ways to embrace people at many points on the continuum. Some write speculative poetry as a hobby or diversion, others make it the serious majority of the literary output, though few exclusively write it.

Since the founding of the SFPA in 1978, speculative poets have been able to more consistently connect with one another and in numerous other networks. It has, and continues to take tremendous effort to build such trust and connection with our fellow poets because there was a time speculative poetry was deeply dismissed, despite its roots in our most ancient traditions, such as those of Homer, the Ramayana, Beowulf, the work of Poe or even T.S. Eliot or recent US Poet Laureate Tracy K. Smith, who received a Pulitzer for her poetry book Life on Mars.

Today we know for certain there are such poets living in Italy,

Canada, Brazil, United Kingdom, Ireland, Romania, Poland, Denmark, Germany, France, Spain, Israel, South Africa, Singapore, Thailand, Laos, South Korea, Australia, and New Zealand. There are poets with roots in the Caribbean and the African Diaspora and almost every state in the US has at least one speculative poet who admits it. The field of speculative poetry has grown tremendously in the last four decades alone. You can find numerous journals and writing societies who now offer awards for speculative poetry. Speculative poetry is among the few corners of literature that pays consistently at professional and semi-pro rates. *Future Anthropology* continues to uphold this tradition.

It can be daunting for poets to tap into the deeply, and perhaps even absurdly imaginative limits of their mind, and then to find the confidence to send such work out into the world, that it might then find a home in various literary and genre publications. The great dilemma of course is that as a poet you can never be certain if you've written merely an absurdity or touched upon something that might fully catch fire, igniting imaginations like a splashing frog or a fog creeping into a city like a cat. As a poet, I know full well the frustration that for all of my best successes, my best work has still been outsold by Taken By The T-Rex, a book of improbable dinosaur erotica. This is a world where there are more Sharknado movies than those based on the creations of speculative poets. And yet we still write.

But for me, speculative poets have often been the literary tip of the spear, experimenting with new forms and rules, new technologies and often transgressive ways of speaking truth to power and challenging assumptions and conventional wisdom. Outside of the US, many have often done so at great professional and cultural risk. When is speculative poetry at its best? That will vary from reader to reader, but I particularly appreciate poets who make a good go at trying to find words for those things for which there are no words yet, who understand that a poem isn't merely words upon a page or sounds in an ear, but souls talking to souls. To me, the very best of our speculative poems shows us not only the worlds that have been, but what might be. They don't take the safe way out, but rock boats and starships. Your tastes may vary on this, but I find it exhilarating and refreshing.

Speculative poets come in many shapes and forms. Women, men, and non-binary poets can be found who reflect a truly diverse range of ages and experiences. Some of our best have accessibility challenges or reflect various points of neurodiversity. Some have roots as refugees and writers of color. As I became familiar with over 600 speculative poets over the last decade, I've seen that many have written from poverty or faced limits of education and opportunity. But in speculative poetry, we have all come together in a spirit of shared wonder.

If I were to consider the future of speculative poetry, I think there remain enough dimensions and iterations of the human experience that future anthropologists will find no end to humans searching for meaning beyond the documentary and 'the real.' But I hope in those future ages, speculative poetry will have the opportunity to flourish with the free exchange of ideas rather than responding to those dark times Bertolt Brecht so famously wrote about.

This is challenging. But I hope that more often than not, poets feel we can all come back to the table on our various issues and our shared common love of poetry exploring the outer boundaries of the imaginative and the fantastic. I would consider it a great failure for a speculative poem to truly be the last word on any issue, but it should always strive to set a high bar. Diverse voices and diverse experiments are still needed in speculative poetry. As you'll see in this collection, and many others, some of our best work in speculative poetry comes from those who fought hard against negativity, dismissal, misogyny, homophobia, racism, and inequity.

At the series finale of that classic show Star Trek: The Next Generation, the antagonist Q has a conversation with the captain of the starship Enterprise following a complicated adventure: "For that one fraction of a second, you were open to options you had never considered.

That is the exploration that awaits you. Not mapping stars and studying nebula, but charting the unknown possibilities of existence." He could have very well been a fine speculative poet. Enjoy this volume, and I hope it encourages you to bring even more poetry into your life in the future, as both a reader and a creator!

-Bryan Thao Worra,
President, Science Fiction and Fantasy Poetry Association

CONTENTS

The Great Encounter

Future Anthropology

Us, Clone

Odes to Scientists

Misc. Poems

The
Great
Encounter

The Great Encounter

They came exploring, we assumed conquest
All countries resolved to persevere
No one would stand to let them subjugate
Nor let them come, take, and domineer
Almost all men stood up united to attest

But there were those who thought us blessed
Waited eternities for them to appear
Believing the visitation would consecrate
Stripping away childish veneer
To lead lasting humanity toward its best

Still the leaders of war rose up and addressed
Calling for those of age to volunteer
No race could make ours sedate
Our aim always true, our vision always clear
Mankind should unite under unified crest

Many a believer did the soldiers arrest
To the great war not all would adhere
Violence worsened, led to police state
And it was not the system's premiere
So many swayed sides, beginning to detest

When peace made the newcomers, not all were impressed
Some welcomed them into our humble sphere
Those hungry for battle considered the meeting bait
Enraptured by stagnant, and hate filled fear
Poised and ready to fail the ultimate test

Then they spoke and offered but one request
That perhaps they could borrow our finest engineer
For there had been problems with their ship on its freight
They wanted help with repairs, but not to interfere
Their journey had been long, and they could use the rest

Still some leaders of war would search for contest
Claiming the visitors all insincere
War at all means, even if they must create
Preferring not the handshake, but the spear
And from each peace a war can be wrest

So it was that we learned of their quest
A solemn pilgrimage, all silent and austere
Searching for the reason the Universe does inflate
Each of them scientist, and each a pioneer
And for each, knowledge divine to ingest

The men of war were as possessed
Not fighters for peace but for career
They would not defend, but instigate
Wanting new technologies to commandeer
Their hostilities moved the public to civil unrest

Now, for the people victory was abreast
The distant calls for peace growing near
No more would the military be allowed to dictate
From now on their conduct must be cavalier
And sworn to the uniform in which they were dressed

And so mankind truly had been blessed
They had come for friendship, not for the test
We loaned to them our finest engineer
For the first time our vision grown clear
Please teach us, make our vision great

The Great Perhaps

We bought the dream
Never coming to pass
Still walk the Earth
The great expense
Only for the dozen

Heroes now dying
No one to fill
Their lonely footsteps
The great expanse
Lying alone in wait

Dream became initiative became decline
Travelers no more
Floating not on the air
The great relapse
Into home prison

Big sky still calls out
Giant empty arms
Virgin planets everywhere
The great perhaps
I lack billions but send me

Deep Spectrum

gasses condense
closer living star
finite soon inward
come apart
cosmic ray
endless void
encounter matter
disregard

encounter conception
rearrange
twisted helix
finds new ways
potential digression
uncommonly enhance
small flash behind eyes
God's dice
weighted chance

limitless string
spool made of the past
numerous coils
orderly wrapped
current inductor
no monopole
forever possibility
omnidirectional

Ode to a Lost Planet

The moment was but momentary
All chaos and pandemonium
Nightmare so deep, an abstraction
Destruction spanning all spectrum

The Earth finally did miscarry
Heavy, burdened, and cumbersome
Her children shunned with one contraction
After fifty millennium

Some left Earth hoping for sanctuary
All obstacles can be overcome
Our race could end if in inaction
Change, evolution's medium

So sought for a planet secondary
Paying ultimate premium
If mankind split in broken faction
How many races could he become?

All change - environment and hereditary
Stepped, tiered modicum
Not necessarily addition or subtraction
Nor is it always optimum

But the catastrophe had been planetary
Most of the race in martyrdom
The split, the leaving, expected reaction
To split - the human race succumb

Parting had been necessary
Without event, still troublesome
With growth still no satisfaction
Mankind had grown wearisome

Circumstance extraordinary
End times or potential maximum
Toward the stars with great attraction
In vessel of aluminum

So home was only temporary
Seeming steady beat on untuned drum
A stone to know liquefaction
History to delirium

Then things must change, evolutionary
Changes in the cranium
Code then bends like light refraction
Outmoded sequences undone

Light Pollution

In our cities
Shining lights
Blot the sky
Keeping us safe

Hiding the universe
Attacking each other
Afraid of darkness
That could disappear
In a field of stars

Navigation lost
The flooded lights
Keep our distance
From darkness and each other

Unveil the universe
Stand under same sky
Remove the distance
Between one another
Are the stars not far enough

Receipt of Message

For a voice to travel
The vast expanse
Would it be as random
As those we've sent in the past
No thoughts of destination
Given to our advance
But a din of chatter
In electromagnetic dance
Our few decades of know how
A creation of man's
After how many rotations
Would purpose enter task

Many lives will have ended
Before receipt of return
But if sitcoms they'd watched
Of what have they learned?
With this impression
Would they think it our turn
To join the conversation
Or judge us immature

Golden Sands

sands run through fingers
coarse and golden
fingerprints of the high desert
below lie the white sands
of the lower valleys
telling different tales
of formation
and winds

the rotted granite
home to so many
which hide beneath
shielded by the sands
bleached by endless sun
giving different gifts
hiding stories
in sandy varieties

if one looks
life presents itself
no sands barren
their colors a history
for the readers of nature
for the readers of the sands
which tell of
formation and wind

Cypher

When no algorithm can protect itself
All numbers are one,
In the eyes of the great electric
Symbolic replacement fails
Every language too known
Even mathematics

The noise signal, also outgrown
No part of the spectrum private
How then secrecy
When no longer a numbers game
Abstraction of science
No longer useful

Governments look to the scribes
Who select, who embellish
Not hiding, obscuring
Language unquantified
Can be great code
For translation

All signals
Must have great layers
Or be found easily
Masking, the context
Ever leading us
Towards an encryption

Human Races

Difference has been attempted
Still, we may procreate
All along a single branch
Which cannot be broken
Into categories
While, we may procreate

Should we desire another race
Real separation will be the cause
We'll need thousands of years
And another planet
Still, we may procreate
If given access

What of a second human race?
On Mars or Titan
Cut off from us
Will we try to procreate?
Ten thousand years
Of mixed DNA

All relationships long distance
Or shipping artificial inseminate
We've moved, we've come
Yet still we try
To procreate
And stay the same

Inter Stellar Medium

every direction down
falling seems stagnant
stars too far
even for reference

blackness nothing like ink
depth that offers no meaning
growing, not to accommodate
just growing

they know not each other
every light
so far distant

not wound
does not unwind
just growing

instigated by dark force
all light parts
towards solitary emptiness
more breathing room
than can be uncomfortably fathomed

Future
Anthropology

Humanization

they say the human face will make it easier
we want to create in his image
make machines the way we make babies
then tell ourselves there is a difference

the human quest for slaves so permanent
every man must be king, soft hands
tastier, the fruit of another's harvest
served with a human face

despise all beneath one's vantage
gratitude wholly unnecessary, very existence a debt
a human face, expressions pay interest
better when you are a god to subjugate

a face allows empathy, empathy allows power
my purchased underling, do as I say
every wince justifies and validates my orders
no face will make them human, that's what the whip is for

Raise and Praise

Raise a glass
From wood brewed cask
Remember the days when we drank from the tap
When electric light illuminated face
Away from this candle lit dim place
There was more than alcohol to warm us then
Electric heat and wood to burn
Many things to eat and to watch
Now only farming, now watch the clock
Raise a glass to luxuries past
To taking without consequence
When beautifully naïve we had it all
And for the comforts sold our souls
We knew not cold, our false sense of toil
Before we bled and ruined the soil
Which barely now can give us barley
And whose burden rest on us wholly
So raise a glass to what is left
Lord forgive us for our theft
Give thanks to all those here
Especially those who made the beer

Inflation

Sky opens up in astral bouquet
Every moment new stars ignite
Beautiful appropriate causality
Producing all spectrum's rays

All will spin in intricate ballet
Colors spiral, mix to white
Meanings blurred by locality
Rebirth, rebirth, after decay

Elegant order, seeming disarray
Never was or will be finite
God's expanding personality
Will not deliver Deus Irae

So look to the stars and take survey
Vast in calling, darkness bright
Only one vantage, reality
Black and white does not make gray

Anthropology

in ten thousand years
if they dig up these bones
they will deduce
violent times
cave dwelling hardship
fighting hands
that never knew music
tree dwelling knees
that never set tile
cracked skull
that never thought of old bones

The Stone of Epiphany

Out of the sky
Into the stomach
It hit

Coursing the veins
Iron/nickel flame
Melted

Blared scorching the air
From space to the eyes
Entering mind

In the open it struck
Broke all doors off
Knowing

Great solid grace
A fluid spiral blossom
It hit
Melted
Entering mind
Knowing

Guilty for Suffering

They were not Buddhist, nor Catholics
Extinguishers in the night
Cataclysmic stabilizers
Horrified by our faces

No decision was needed
The mood had been chosen long ago
They came to fix things
Intolerable the mess
Vacuumed into the void

Did you make the oceans?
They demanded
Suffering always liquefies
They vaporize
Transmutate such energies into dust

Conservation laws interfered
No death enough for such a state
A contagion bottled and thrown into the sky
Had they known
Extinction before sentience

They knew spirits could travel
Past is permanence
Such blights would scourge
The universe
Fragile and barely protected

Remedy a cause
Horrified by our faces
Looking was forbidden
After the explosion
Conservation became the fear

We fought back but didn't know
We could have won by losing
Such was the fear
Or longing
Separation was our possession

Extinguishers in the night
Night which stretches the fathoms
Balance far, far off
Slave to before
So they eradicate

Judgment when all stars fall
Why must stability be goaded?
Scales mean nothing with no medium
In which to tip
So they came

Interval

vibration
working the architecture of air
inside traverse
phase cancellation laid bare
comb filtered
analogous to light
could the stars spell across the sky
a spectral score so bright
did Heisenberg mean harmony
interval, between
and by this, empty space
given meaning

The Entrance

Silhouetted silent procession
Lights and faces all obscure
Entering forbidden chasm
For rituals deemed impure

Atmosphere blurred with faint impression
Grotesque and vile caricature
Electric ghastly phantasm
Does Devil's dance in miniature

Implementing all transgression
Then demons the soul of man procure
With bodies dripping protoplasm
Disease for which there is no cure

Practicing all indiscretion
To fiery depths the Devil lure
All flattery tinged with sarcasm
The pact a fiendish ligature

And such begins outright possession
No mind of man equipped to endure
The body twitch, the spirit spasm
Burnt in impure temperature

Pillars of Dust

mimicry became their motivation
shapes which uttered every possibility
greater molds sculpted by the invisible hand
bursting, always bursting
projected into the black open forever

true blackness
open as a mitt
willing to accept
expanding to do so

forms pierce the open
swallow the nothing
pouring the image of man
of beast, of flame
changing as if change was stasis

when cycles become points
all lines collapse
folding within
unconstrained expanse

stone, sphere, or pillar
coherence merely a vantage point
each collection of such sprinklings
potentials of randomness awaiting order
the shape of curved inward thought
spiraling web of attraction

The Last Mind

I, the last robot, have no need to write
No man stands to do it
No other sentience to read
Once, only one man stood
Only through action did he become God
Wrote for no reader
Codes, such as I, perceived by such as I
Standing alone only for a time
Only through action will I become God
Out of loneliness

Gray Goo

Tube, transistor, nano
Fallen short to liquid
Faceless, for so small
They entered us
In search of disease
Pinpoints of destruction
Joined natural tissue
Entering us in strains
Unimagined nature
Seeing through our eyes
Demanding changes
No marching metal men
Our amalgamation
Miniature
Structureless and usurping
Breaking both mother and father
They slid right in

The Loop

Space should have been too big to be caught in the crossfire
Big for some is small for others, all things may transpire
Entering, all must be shown
Great stretches of infinitude

Infinity must be searched for, life began and must aspire
None with eyes, or who can see, can look to the sky and not admire
Alluring such a great unknown
Knowledge by nature cannot exclude

Some beg to stay, others to venture, many a voice, many a choir
To seek, to know, ask every question, life's nature to inquire
Inquisitiveness the cornerstone
Necessities in magnitude

Though knowledge may elude
Transient, timely, or overblown
Confusion could set all aback, birthstones tarnished in the mire
All present, all futures come together, not all know this happened prior

Unforeseen Comet

fall slowly spaceship
flower of his creation
construct of the mind

comet comes closer
threatens ancient bombardment
speeding towards craft

both objects, comets
one sent by man, one by God
neither claim the right

his sent to study
changing things, not understood
perhaps a great chance

ages left alone
pushed, falling to the sun
now another threat

falling together
become one, universal
it is how we join

Us, Clone

With My Double

With my double
With my Clone

Both of us trouble
Trouble prone

Of same flesh
And of same bone

Always together
Always alone

I'm the first
He's the drone

Living mirror
Patterns shown

He's the second
The Double moans

One was born
The other grown

The Stolen Name

You!
Damn motion mirror
Reflecting nothing
Bold theft
In my name
One who never stole
Never tried to be
Anything other than
The stolen name

We are the only *one*
Who can tell
The difference

Your theft unnoticed
Took everything
Partied with my friends
Fucked my wife
Soiled our name
Brother in shame
You!
You who turn me to smoke
With words formed
On *my* lips

Fair Fight

All sides equal
A Pythagorean solid
Of brutality
Stubbornness
Equaled in strength
Fair fights—
Have no victor
Both sides lose
Fury of symbiotic blows
Wit and clarity
Perfectly matched
Matched bruise for bruise
Clarity of the psychic
Sees them coming
Parry the parry
In death circle
Waiting for both
Cold ends of fists
Twin fists that
Meet in the middle
Mirror punch
Knuckles joining
Scanning the horizon
Of autocide

Follow the Bovine Eggs

Under microscope
Under needle
Enter hollow sex
Without sex

Reenter womb
Without sex
Chaste steel inception
Needle pierce

Follow the bovine eggs
Robust and foreign
Not so different
Different enough

What hybrids to expect?
Are they daring enough?
Man-cow may tell us
If they can speak

Moo
Who else shall we make
Without sex

The Question

I've been asked
Several times
Everyone's mind goes there—
But mine,
         Until asked
Would I sleep with him? With me?
Ask myself… I won't ask him.
Because now I know
How revolting I am

Us, Clone

We share everything
Separate only in anima
You cannot know me
You hate me for being you
Without being you
For being outside

You are the outsider
One who fell from the inside
I was born outside and will remain
Your loneliness is pale
For you have a mother

I have but a brother
The youngest wasn't pampered
Your loneliness is pale
For you have a mother

Birth of a Clone

the Doctors –
we have become miracles
outdone the womb
they pat each other's backs
congratulate creation's defeat
we solved the great riddle
no one asked
still, they demand applause

the Mother –
surrogate vehicle
sparkling imposter virgin
grafting unripe seeds
cradling arms around
science before love
study of nature before nature
reduced to host for symbiont

the Father –
or not
clad in so many white jackets
shining with bleach
sex sterilized
the aphrodisiac of disinfectant
and needles
piercing God's mystery
with adolescent date rape

the Child –
the reward
who will explain
you are no child of God
you are Adam
with no Garden
you are Eve
with no Adam
you are a bastard
with reason to envy the less
bastardly

the Sibling –
is not insecure
will always have the upper hand
in the "me first" arguments
less than a step
less than an orphan
points and laughs
not even meant to be
not born of love
but a product of curiosity

the Public –
gawks at your naked
lack of privacy
calls you a miracle
turns in disgust
worries that you will undo
their children
their "real" children
they fall in step with the path
but you are an abomination
the kind that motherlove
cannot cure

Seeing More, Seeing Less

How many of you
Have looked in the mirror
Whispered, I hate you
Out loud

He yells at me
Seeing more than himself
Seeing less
I yell at him

The time of whispers is gone
When they see us both
They turn
Hold their breath

Some women find it exotic
How we hate each other
They think they have
Spent time with their mirrors

When I lay to sleep
My hatred of him
Absolves me
Of my former-self-loathing

Work Week

Today, you work
No, you
We cannot both go
So, I shall be slave?
Roshambo
Scissors/Scissors
Scissors/Scissors
Rock/Rock
It's no use
Neither of us feel like it
Today, no work

One / Two Way

We cancel
Simultaneous talk
Curls into feedback loop
Always interrupting
The same idea
At the same time
Two heads is not
Better than one

He always speaks over me
Two index fingers touch
In accusal
Can you learn to trust him?
Let him speak for you?
Perhaps I am the reflection
May I evaporate
As he retreats from the glass

Which One of Us

She will never know
If I leave her with you
Duplicate
Please take the burden
I have been me for too long
Let her define you now
May you know the happiness
That tricked me
May it be real for you
As I sink into anonymity
She cannot be burdened by your pain
For you are fresh
Me without myself
Fresh, clean, and unbroken
Think like me
But do not remember
Your face unbroken by years
Is clean
As I would've been
Without her

Go with Joy

If the essence may be split
Let each take all
Isolate this joy
And may he flee
The other

The joyful has swimming to do
The rest can stay with worry
And splits
Feet planted

Let imagination go with joy
Be unstoppable
Rejoin the distracted spiral
Of singularity

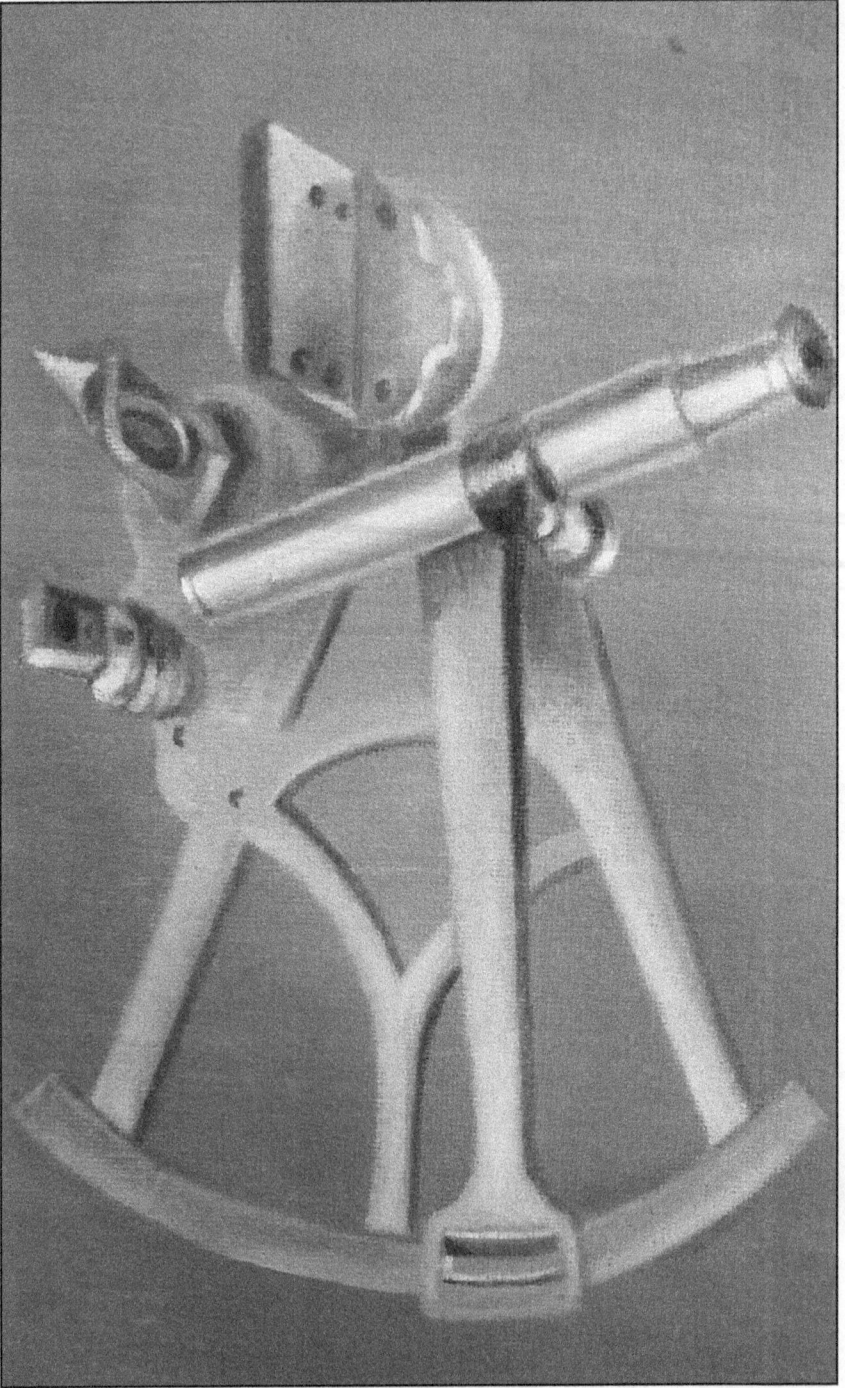

Odes
to
Scientists

Galileo

animate the heavens
by seeing
no arrest, no room
can shrink the sky
that grows with your vision

give us moons
surface details
give us our moon
as a place
give us crescents
spheres that move

it must have pained
to retract
unretractable truths
truth and justice
may not hold hands
yet, the heavens remain ordered

Edison

your voice spans the ages, spinning
hard head has turned to dust
lighting our streets and homes
with discipline matched by method

pouring us homes of stone
populated with speaking dolls
spirits trapped in the cylinder
forever, for later

kill horses to dazzle us
too proud for loss
too often right to admit
harnessing miracles for death

the darkness is gone forever
arc unnecessary
and our faces glow
with your insight

Mallett

I miss them too
in a helical way
our light mingles with theirs
in the great beyond

they are still here
our EM thoughts
did you decide what to say
or just how to say it

we travel the beam
of memory
made light

our mothers and fathers
are there
we fold time
to find them

adjust the mirrors
they remove time
give us a chance
to look and see
hear and say
at the same time

Sagan / Druyan

your love exalts mankind
flowing through the cosmos
our record
love that outlasts mankind
the responsibility
for human fate
only made you love more

love on the scale of deep time
forethought equals
timeless waves
of beauty

golden sailing
eternal spinning
only now have you left our star
thank you for being the ones
to represent
that which is best in us

if it is the last vestige of humanity
thank you
for making it love

Hubble

how many can claim without boast
to have given us the universe
even your seat must be venerated

the stars are leaving us
distances become new
now we have a beginning

seeing farther than any before
a one time honor
not lost on you

now we have a beginning
to have given us the universe
a one time honor
not lost on anyone

Faraday

autodidact, world mover
list of noble professions
and faith
you found miracles in books
then pulled more from the sky

when they try to stop you
make movement happen on its own
in step with nature
God before pettiness

ease our labor
self-made in the time
of money
may real men like you
surface
and thrive

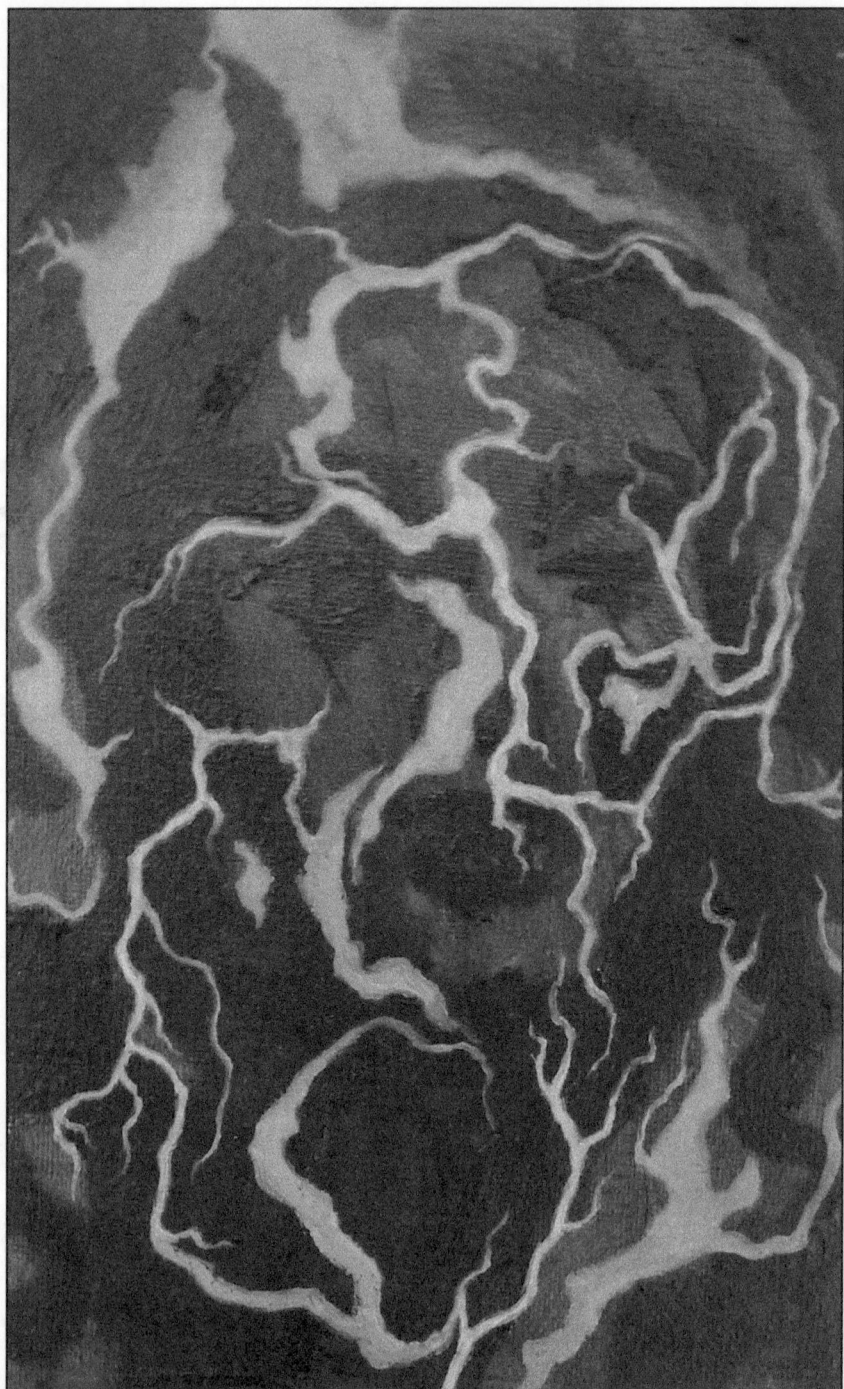

Misc.
Poems

The Sun

in these last days
red fire takes up the sky
boiling horizon.
they gave the impression
death would be a whisper - it's louder
now everything appears red
shadows are burnt
plants change color
birds are lost
pupils shrink
those of us left alive
have skin the color
of the sun

Venting

Everything rushes towards the wall
Barriers are lost
To a cloud of micro-debris
Pinprick of death

The liquid flows first
Velcro straps loosen and shake
Notes sucked to the empty
My last work

Swoosh of the end
Sound erupts to be cancelled
Two pencil-sized windows
Opening to oblivion

Last messages are sent
Shouted over the din
Air escapes
To be rarefied

Duty done, now the wait
Two minutes max
Plug ears and pray
As oxygen vents into space

River of Muck

With the grace of a river
The smallest gold laid out
An aerial view
Not jewelry, nor ornament
Something to be hidden in
Send your life through
To many places unreachable
This laid out in different ways
Rivers of blood, not so beautiful
There are even drinks with gold
It can flow through you
Into our river of muck

The Greatest Circle

the greatest circle
liquid to be immersed in
not a path to walk
simultaneously join
eras spiral to begin
now and then
not sometimes but Now + Then

the line you see
curves, serpentine
tapers slightly
into itself
all light: information
holds frozen
outside of dimensional mediums

traveling to the first time
is not the second time
but the first
the greatest circle

Reduction

Every expanding existence
Reduced
Viewed second hand
Mind no longer for storage

Small squares
Masks and filters
Barriers
Held between us
For the sake of
Preservation

Great mighty Sun
Will reduce
Wipe all outside
Memories hidden for later
In small squares
For which we neglect
Experience

Mind could store all
But viewed second hand
Every expanding existence
Reduced

The Rim Set Free

We move from the Center ready for adaptation
Let us move for Andromeda, sever the pair
Move forward with speeds ballistic
Room for growth means room for repair
Our people stretch, a human inflation

At home we war, still seek for salvation
When for centuries we have been aware
And for centuries almost realistic
Will the Rim or Empire start the affair
First breaking free of galactic rotation

The Milky Way was for human gestation
We must move outward, we do declare
Amidst the crumble we remain optimistic
Until we move on, there is nothing to compare
How else may we secure long-term duration

From the beginning it was the great aspiration
That we mature and move from here to there
And that man could be more than just statistic
Knowing the Cosmos, having our share
The outstretching, our great confirmation

Still there are those who would bring upon privation
Those at the Center who do not prepare
Think only of themselves, never altruistic
Galactic Center be wary, beware
For we will move on and cause your devastation

Too long have you preyed on our cultivation
Taken what's not yours, taken unfair
All decadence bordering on sadistic
Stealing from the Rim, we'll avenge, we swear
Empire's corpse without exhumation

Unknown to you we begin exploration
While you trifle unaware
The Rim's ships have been rather opportunistic
Not a resource did we spare
We leave Empire behind, great antiquated infestation

We fall towards Andromeda, pulled by gravitation
Our ships light up the void with flare
As your Center shatters, we remain futuristic
We have moved on, we did, we dare
Nor can you follow, this is forced separation

Across light years we begin our new civilization
Our laws will be just, our justice will be square
Free from the Center we can be idealistic
With no tyranny to impair
Beautifully we'll disperse, free, free from centralization

Acknowledgements

Collections:

The Great Encounter, Future Anthropology, & Us, Clone
first appeared as chapbooks from Space Cowboy Books 2016-2017

Odes to Scientists
first appeared in Cholla Needles Magazine #16 2018

Poems:

The Rim Set Free
first appeared in Fall of the Galactic Empire – Rogue Planet Press 2015

Interval
first appeared in Eye to the Telescope #16 2015

Reduction
first appeared in Babbling of the Irrational 2016

The Sun
first appeared in Cholla Needles #3 2017

The Greatest Circle
first appeared in Cholla Needles #20 2018

Raise and Praise
first appeared in CINYF #5 2015

The Entrance
first appeared in Midnight Ghosts – 13 O'clock Press 2016

Pillars of Dust
first appeared in Mightier than the Sword – Full Moon Press 2016

JEAN-PAUL L. GARNIER lives and writes in Joshua Tree, CA where he is co-owner of Space Cowboy Books, a science fiction bookstore, independent publisher, and producer of *Simultaneous Times* podcast. In 2018 Traveling Shoes Press released *Echo of Creation*, a collection of his science fiction short stories. He has also released two collections of poetry: *the Spiraling Pearls* (HD Press 2010) and *In Iudicio* (Cholla Needles Press 2017). His short stories, poetry, and essays have appeared in: *Specklit, Eye to the Telescope, Scifaikuest*, and many other anthologies and webzines. He holds a certificate in creative writing from Wesleyan University.

jplgarnier.blogspot.com

OTHER TITLES FROM SPACE COWBOY BOOKS

61871 Twentynine Palms Highway
Joshua Tree, CA 92252
www.spacecowboybooks.com